ICONIC NATIONAL PARKS

ROCKY MOUNTAIN NATIONAL PARK

BY HEATHER C. HUDAK

Core Library

An Imprint of Abdo Publishing
abdobooks.com

Cover image: More than 90 percent of Rocky Mountain National Park is designated wilderness.

abdobooks.com

Published by Abdo Publishing, a division of ABDO, PO Box 398166, Minneapolis, Minnesota 55439.

Printed in the United States of America, North Mankato, Minnesota.
052025
092025

Cover Photo: Wayne Boland/Moment Open/Getty Images
Interior Photos: benedek/E+/Getty Images, 4–5; Red Line Editorial, 7; John Couture/Shutterstock Images, 10–11; ilbusca/DigitalVision Vectors/Getty Images, 14; Denver Public Library/Bridgeman Images, 16; Carlos A. Carreno/c3.photos/Moment/Getty Images, 18–19; Colin D. Young/Alamy, 20; iStockphoto, 23, 40 (fire, binoculars), 40 (car), 40 (bag), 40 (plant), 40 (mountain); Danita Delimont/Shutterstock Images, 25; Shutterstock Images, 26–27, 40 (dogs), 43 (bottom); Sean Xu/Shutterstock Images, 28; Stephen Moehle/Shutterstock Images, 31, 45; Christopher M. Hall/Shutterstock Images, 32; Helen H. Richardson/MediaNews Group/Denver Post/Getty Images, 34–35; Takako Phillips/iStockphoto, 36; Brian Welker/Alamy, 42 (top); Hale Kell/Shutterstock Images, 42 (middle); National Park Service, 42 (bottom); Colin D. Young/Shutterstock Images, 43 (top); Kelly vanDellen/Shutterstock Images, 43 (middle)

Editor: Christa Kelly
Series Designer: Marley Richmond

Library of Congress Control Number: 2024949001

Publisher's Cataloging-in-Publication Data

Names: Hudak, Heather C., author.
Title: Rocky Mountain National Park / by Heather C. Hudak
Description: Minneapolis, Minnesota: Abdo Publishing, 2026 | Series: Iconic national parks | Includes online resources and index.
Identifiers: ISBN 9781098297190 (lib. bdg.) | ISBN 9798384919711 (ebook)
Subjects: LCSH: Rocky Mountain National Park (Colo.)--Juvenile literature. | Mountain ranges--Juvenile literature. | Natural monuments--Juvenile literature. | Scenic landscapes--Juvenile literature. | National parks and reserves--Juvenile literature.
Classification: DDC 978.8--dc23

CONTENTS

CHAPTER ONE

ADVENTURES FOR EVERYONE

Charlotte and her family were taking a road trip. After nearly two days of driving, they reached their first stop. Charlotte stepped out of the SUV into Rocky Mountain National Park in Colorado.

Moraine Park Campground would be their home base for the next four nights. Charlotte looked around. Her breath caught as she took in her surroundings. Longs Peak, the park's highest mountain, towered above her, and the sun shone across the ponderosa pine forest.

More than four million people visit Rocky Mountain National Park each year.

PERSPECTIVES

TOURISM HOTSPOT

Visitors need a reservation to enter Rocky Mountain National Park during the peak tourist season. This prevents overcrowding. Nature photographer Erik Stensland says, "Crowds can completely change our experience of a national park, making it stressful and feel like we're back in the city, when we really come out here to connect with the natural world, to enjoy the solitude, the silence, the birds singing, the rivers running. It's a magical experience—if you can get away from the crowds."

Her family's first stop was the Alpine Visitor Center. It was the starting point for the Alpine Ridge Trail. Her family grabbed their water bottles and started hiking.

As they climbed higher, Charlotte found it harder to breathe. But the panoramic views at the top were worth all the huffing and puffing to get there. Charlotte looked at the view in awe. If the next destination on their road trip was anything like Rocky Mountain National Park, it would be an unforgettable experience.

ROCKY MOUNTAIN NATIONAL PARK

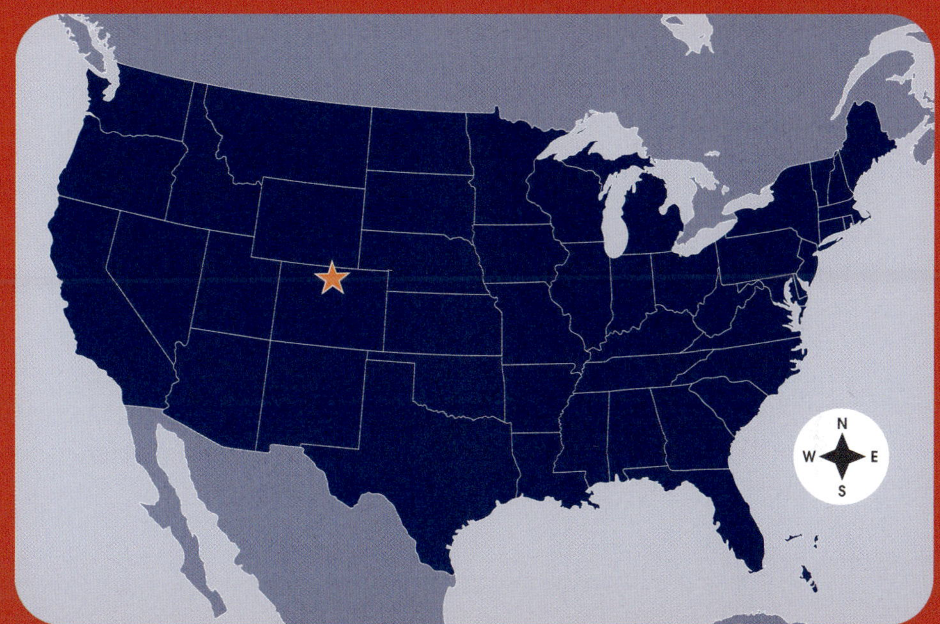

Rocky Mountain National Park is located in north-central Colorado in the Southwestern United States. It is about a two-hour drive from Denver, the capital of Colorado. How do you think the park's location contributes to its popularity?

AN ICONIC PARK

Rocky Mountain National Park is one of the most visited parks in the United States. The park protects 415 square miles (1,075 sq km) of north-central Colorado. The Continental Divide cuts through the park, making way for spectacular landscapes. Deep valleys,

CONTINENTAL DIVIDE

A continental divide is a natural boundary that separates the river systems within a continent. The Continental Divide of the Americas runs through the middle of Rocky Mountain National Park. Rivers to the west of the divide flow into the Pacific Ocean. Rivers to the east flow into the Gulf of Mexico. About 42 miles (68 km) of the divide cuts through Rocky Mountain National Park. This is just a small portion of the Continental Divide, which spans nearly the entire length of North and South America.

thick evergreen forests, colorful wildflower meadows, large expanses of tundra, and shimmering alpine lakes dot the land. Towering over the park is the stunning Southern Rocky Mountain range.

Rocky Mountain National Park is an extraordinary place for people to explore the great outdoors. Breathtaking views, amazing wildlife, and historical artifacts offer something for everyone to enjoy. A visit to this iconic national park is a truly unforgettable adventure.

STRAIGHT TO THE SOURCE

Each national park makes a foundation document. This document explores the goals, significance, and history of the park. Rocky Mountain National Park's foundation document says:

> *The purpose of Rocky Mountain National Park is to preserve the high-elevation ecosystems and wilderness character of the southern Rocky Mountains within its borders and to provide the freest recreational use of and access to the park's scenic beauties, wildlife, natural features and processes, and cultural objects.*

Source: "Foundation Document: Rocky Mountain National Park." *National Park Service*, May 2013, nps.gov. Accessed 23 Sept. 2024.

WHAT'S THE BIG IDEA?

Read this quote carefully. What is the main idea? How is it supported by details? Why is protecting the Rocky Mountains important?

CHAPTER TWO

HISTORY OF ROCKY MOUNTAIN NATIONAL PARK

The Rocky Mountains are a mountain range stretching from New Mexico to Canada. Rocky Mountain National Park is within the Front Range. This is the easternmost mountain range in the Southern Rocky Mountains.

The Rocky Mountains are unusual. Most mountain ranges are located at the edges of tectonic plates, but the Rocky Mountains are in the middle of a plate. There is little tectonic activity in the area today. However, about

Geologists are fascinated by the Rocky Mountains' strange geology and landscapes.

FROZEN IN TIME

Archaeologists have discovered ancient artifacts frozen in ice patches throughout Rocky Mountain National Park. Long ago, animals came to the ice patches for relief from the summer heat. Ancient peoples came to the ice patches to hunt the wildlife. Wooden items, stone tools, and animal remains have been preserved in excellent condition inside the snow and ice. Many of the objects are between 600 and 4,200 years old. Once exposed to air, they begin to break down, so archaeologists are rushing to find as many artifacts as they can before the ice melts and they are lost forever.

55 to 80 million years ago, tectonic activity caused the earth's crust to fold and break. Huge chunks of rock thrust upward, forming steep peaks. Volcanic activity and erosion from rivers, streams, and other natural forces shaped the land.

About one million years ago, the climate started to cool. Glaciers carved the deep valleys, sheer cliffs, and steep mountains that make up Rocky Mountain National Park. Natural forces continue to shape the landscape.

HUMAN HISTORY

Evidence of the first humans in Rocky Mountain National Park dates back more than 10,000 years. Early hunter-gatherers, or Paleo-Indians, likely followed woolly mammoths to the area. Artifacts from these ancient people have been found in the park.

The challenging terrain made it difficult to live in the region, so Paleo-Indians settled in the nearby plains. Ancient people continued to visit the mountains for seasonal hunting, setting up temporary campsites during warmer times of year. They used present-day Trail Ridge Road to cross the mountains.

Paleo-Indians were the earliest ancestors of the American Indian nations associated with the park. These nations include the Ute, Shoshone, Comanche, and Arapaho. Though none of these nations built permanent settlements in the area, the region provided them with valuable resources.

Spanish explorers and French trappers first visited the area in the 1600s and 1700s. They traded food and

Thousands of people traveled to Colorado after gold was discovered in the region.

horses with American Indians in exchange for meat and hides. In the mid-1800s, gold was discovered in Colorado, and miners rushed to the area. It wasn't long before settlers also moved to the area for its rich natural resources. These settlers stole the American Indians' land.

ESTABLISHING THE PARK

As more people came to the area, the land quickly changed. Trees were cut down for wood. Animals were hunted for sport. Around 1900, future president Theodore Roosevelt and fellow conservationists urged the US government to preserve the land. By 1909, there was growing support for the creation of a national park.

Most local leaders and businesses supported the idea. Enos Mills, a local nature guide and naturalist, worked to draw attention to the cause. He gave speeches across the

PERSPECTIVES

AMERICAN INDIANS AND THE ROCKY MOUNTAINS

For thousands of years, American Indians have cared for the land that is now part of Rocky Mountain National Park. Many believe that the park does not educate visitors enough about the park's native people. Betsy Chapoose is a member of the Ute nation. She says, "I would like people to know . . . that there are people who still utilize that environment for what we believe in. I want people to know that [the park] is closely related to the Ute people. . . . It's still where our ancestors walked, and it may be our ancestors [who are] helping those plants to grow there."

Enos Mills lived from 1870 to 1922.

United States and wrote letters and articles about protecting the mountain wilderness.

Finally, on January 26, 1915, President Woodrow Wilson signed the Rocky Mountain National Park Act. This act officially established the park. For his role in fighting for the park, Mills became known as the Father of Rocky Mountain National Park.

STRAIGHT TO THE SOURCE

In the early 1900s, Enos Mills led the initiative to establish Rocky Mountain National Park. The following excerpt is from a statement Mills issued in 1909 explaining his reasons for wanting to protect the area:

> *Around Estes Park, Colorado, are mountain scenes of exceptional beauty and grandeur. . . . In many respects this section is losing its wild charms. Extensive areas of primeval forests have been misused and ruined; sawmills are humming and cattle are in the wild gardens! The once numerous big game has been hunted out of existence and the picturesque beaver are almost gone.*

Source: "Chapter II: Enos Mills and the Creation of the Park." *Rocky Mountain Administrative History*, 15 Jan. 2004, nps.gov. Accessed 18 Nov. 2024.

CONSIDER YOUR AUDIENCE

Adapt this passage for a different audience, such as your friends or family. Write a blog post conveying this same information for the new audience. How does your post differ from the original text and why?

CHAPTER THREE

PLANTS AND ANIMALS

Rocky Mountain National Park's diverse landscapes provide homes for a wide range of wildlife. More than 1,000 species of plants live in the park. Many animals also call the park home, including 60 mammal species, nearly 300 bird species, and several reptile, amphibian, and fish species.

The park's plants and animals are spread throughout various ecosystems. Each species is adapted to live in different areas

Early morning and early evening are the best times to spot wildlife in the park.

Between 300 and 400 bighorn sheep live in Rocky Mountain National Park.

and elevations. Many visitors come to the park to see these fascinating species.

MONTANE ECOSYSTEM

The Rocky Mountain's montane ecosystem starts at about 5,600 feet (1,700 m) above sea level and extends to roughly 9,500 feet (2,900 m). This ecosystem contains rivers, open meadows, and hills. It has the widest range of plant and animal species of all the ecosystems in the park. Some of the most common montane plants include ponderosa pines, grasses, sagebrush, mountain mahogany, and wildflowers such as mountain iris and blue columbine. Animals found in this ecosystem include western tanagers, Steller's jays, bighorn sheep, black bears, mule deer, garter snakes, and porcupines.

Abert's squirrels are some of the easiest wildlife to spot in the montane ecosystem. They are found mainly on the park's eastern edge, nesting in the ponderosa pines. Squirrels play a key role in keeping the park healthy. They are prey for larger animals in the park, such as owls, coyotes, and red foxes. They also scatter and bury seeds. This helps new plants grow.

GLOBAL IMPORTANCE

In 1976, the United Nations Educational, Scientific and Cultural Organization (UNESCO) named Rocky Mountain National Park an international biosphere reserve. Biosphere reserves are known for their diverse plants and animals and outstanding natural environments. The park was also recognized by Audubon as a Global Important Bird Area in 2000. It provides diverse habitats for many bird species.

SUBALPINE ECOSYSTEM

The subalpine ecosystem begins around 9,000 feet (2,750 m) and rises to about 11,000 feet (3,350 m). The area is known for its thick forests. Subalpine summers are short and cool, and winters are long and cold.

The Engelmann spruce, subalpine fir, and limber pine are some of the most common tree species in subalpine forests. These trees can become stunted and twisted at higher elevations. Animals in the region include mountain lions, long-tailed weasels, meadow voles, and snowshoe hares.

PERSPECTIVES

RESPECT THE WILDLIFE

While the animals at Rocky Mountain National Park may be cute, they are also wild and unpredictable. Visitors should give the park's wildlife plenty of space. This keeps both visitors and animals safe. Park ranger Neil Coen says, "Respect wildlife. People always want to feed the animals because they're cute. They want to take one home in a box. We've had people feed the squirrels and lead them into their vehicle."

In the summer, long-tailed weasels have brown fur. In the winter, they grow white coats.

ALPINE TUNDRA ECOSYSTEM

Rocky Mountain National Park has one of the largest protected alpine tundra ecosystems in the continental United States. It covers about one-third of the park. The alpine tundra starts at about 11,000 feet (3,350 m) and reaches the top of the Longs Peak at 14,259 feet (4,346 m). Only plants and animals adapted to the extreme cold, high winds, and intense sunshine live in this ecosystem.

No trees can survive in the alpine tundra. Instead, the region is home to grasses, flowers, lichens, and mosses. These plants are small and grow close to the warm soil to keep from freezing. Many plants, such as alpine forget-me-nots, have hairs or wax on their buds, stems, and leaves to protect them from the elements. Some plants, such as alpine clovers, have hardy stems that anchor them to the ground in high winds.

Nearly 20 mammal species live in the alpine tundra ecosystem year-round. These animals include pikas. Pikas are small mammals with big ears and thick fur. Though the animals resemble rodents, they are related to rabbits. Other species, such as elk, coyotes, bighorn sheep, and mountain lions, visit seasonally and move to lower elevations during the coldest months.

The white-tailed ptarmigan is one of the few bird species adapted to the alpine tundra. These birds have feathers on their legs and feet to protect them from the cold. They burrow into the snow, using it as insulation to stay warm.

White-tailed ptarmigan eat buds, leaves, and seeds.

RIPARIAN ZONES

Riparian zones are wetlands next to rivers or other bodies of fresh water. Plants and animals are abundant in these zones. Riparian plants in the region include willow and cottonwood trees, bog birch, chiming bells, and cow parsnip.

Red-winged blackbirds, boreal toads, and western chorus frogs can be found in the riparian zones of Rocky Mountain National Park. Beavers are also found in the area. This species is especially important. Beavers build dams throughout the park. This creates wetlands that provide food and habitats for many riparian species.

CHAPTER FOUR

RECREATION

No matter the season, Rocky Mountain National Park is a great place for outdoor adventures. The park offers sweeping mountain views, diverse wildlife viewing, and exciting recreation opportunities. In the summer, visitors can experience the park through camping, hiking, fishing, bicycling, and horseback riding. In the winter, tourists can go snowshoeing, sledding, ice climbing, and cross-country skiing.

Rocky Mountain National Park's trails take visitors to lakes, waterfalls, and mountain peaks.

Bear Lake is nearly 10,000 feet (3,000 m) above sea level.

Hiking is one of the most popular activities in Rocky Mountain National Park. The park has more than 355 miles (570 km) of hiking trails that range from flat and easy to steep and mountainous. The hike to Bear Lake is one of the most popular trails in the park. The flat gravel path winds about 0.6 miles (1 km) around the shoreline of Bear Lake. It offers scenic views of Hallett Peak and the surrounding mountains. Bear Lake

Trailhead is also the starting point for other hikes, such as Alberta Falls and Nymph, Dream, and Emerald Lakes.

At 14,259 feet (4,346 m), Longs Peak is the highest mountain in the park. In the summer, thousands of visitors hike the Keyhole Route to the top of Longs Peak. It is a challenging route with narrow ledges, sheer rock faces, steep cliffs, loose rocks, and changing weather conditions. The route to Longs Peak is especially dangerous in winter and should be

CAMPING IN THE PARK

Camping is a great way to connect with nature at Rocky Mountain National Park. There are five campgrounds at the park. Each offers a different experience. Glacier Basin provides easy access to Bear Lake and its many trails. Longs Peak Campground serves as a base camp for those planning to climb the park's highest mountain. Moraine Park Campground offers beautiful views of Longs Peak and the park's forests. Timber Creek is located alongside the Colorado River. Aspenglen is nestled among pine forests and wildflower meadows and is open year-round.

PERSPECTIVES

LEAVE NO TRACE

One way visitors can help protect and maintain Rocky Mountain National Park is to leave no trace. Visitors should stay on trails to protect the park's plants. Tourists should dispose of all trash, bring everything out of the park that they brought into it, and leave all plants, rocks, and artifacts as they were. "Leave what you find," says park ranger Neil Coen. "People always want to be taking stuff for souvenirs. If everybody's doing that, nothing's left."

attempted only by experienced hikers.

Another way to take in the park's scenery is to drive along Old Fall River Road or Trail Ridge Road. Both routes highlight the park's natural features. Old Fall River Road was the first road into Rocky Mountain National Park. The gravel road gives visitors a taste of what it was like to visit the park in its early days. At more than 12,000 feet (3,700 m), Trail Ridge Road is the highest paved road in the US national park system. Approximately 11 miles (18 km) of the road is above the tree line, making Rocky Mountain the only

Old Fall River Road offers beautiful panoramic views of Rocky Mountain National Park.

national park where visitors can drive across the alpine tundra region.

EXPERIENCE THE ANIMALS

There are many ways to enjoy the wildlife at Rocky Mountain National Park. Fishing is a popular activity. Visitors can fish at more than 50 lakes and streams throughout the park. In the winter, tourists can try ice fishing.

Hundreds of mule deer live in Rocky Mountain National Park.

Wildlife watching is another popular activity at Rocky Mountain National Park. Many visitors rank it as the top reason to visit. The park's vast wilderness attracts many large animals.

Mule deer are some of the most common animals in the park. They can be seen in all parts of the park, but they are most often found in open areas at low elevations. Elk are easy to spot year-round in the park's meadows and at the edges of forests. In the winter, as many as 800 elk live in the park. The park is also home to bighorn sheep, which are often found at Sheep Lakes from May through mid-August. A small number of moose roam the willow thickets along the Colorado River in the Kawuneeche Valley.

Visitors should always view the park's wildlife from a safe distance. Getting too close can put humans and animals in danger. It's important to stay at least 75 feet (23 m) away from all wildlife and 120 feet (37 m) away from large animals such as bears, moose, and mountain lions. Tourists can use binoculars and cameras to view these animals from afar.

FURTHER EVIDENCE

Chapter Four explores some of the fun things to do in Rocky Mountain National Park. What is the main point of this chapter? What key evidence supports this point? Read the article on the website below. Does the information on the website support the main point of the chapter? Does it present new information?

EVERYTHING TO KNOW ABOUT ROCKY MOUNTAIN NATIONAL PARK

abdocorelibrary.com/rocky-mountain-national-park

CHAPTER FIVE

CARING FOR THE PARK

The National Park Service (NPS) is responsible for preserving the park's natural and cultural resources. In addition to maintaining the park, the NPS must make the park's resources available for people to enjoy. Balancing both of these duties can be tricky.

To address this challenge, NPS park rangers and volunteers take on many different tasks within the park. Some work at visitor centers, trailheads, or historical sites.

Park rangers manage which visitors get to camp and hike in the park's wilderness.

Rocky Mountain National Park has four visitor centers.

They provide educational programs to help visitors better connect with the park. Rangers and volunteers also help repair trails, participate in scientific studies, maintain campsites, rescue climbers, and protect the park's plants and animals.

Other groups work with the NPS to maintain the park. One of these groups is the Rocky Mountain Conservancy. The organization was founded in 1931 to provide educational programs and visitor services for the park. The Conservancy also raises funds for special projects, such as trail improvement, historical site preservation, and land acquirement for the park.

CONCERNS AND CONSERVATION EFFORTS

One of the biggest threats facing Rocky Mountain National Park is climate change. Also known as global warming, climate change is the gradual increase of the earth's temperatures. It affects every aspect of the park's ecosystems. Climate change can lead to shrinking glaciers, increases in

TRAIL RESTORATION

Trails provide access to the most scenic and cherished parts of Rocky Mountain National Park. Due to the large number of visitors to the park, the trails are in constant need of repairs or updates. Since 1985, the Rocky Mountain Conservancy has raised funds for trail projects. Funds have been used to improve the trail from Alberta Falls to Lake Haiyaha and to build accessible trails around Sprague, Lily, and Bear Lakes.

invasive species, and a rise in extreme weather events such as wildfires, droughts, and floods.

In the past 100 years, the park's average annual temperature has increased by about 3.4 degrees Fahrenheit (1.9°C). This has put the park's ecosystems in danger. The winters are shorter and milder while the summers are longer and warmer. This causes the snow to melt earlier, leaving less water for the park's plants and animals during the summer.

Rocky Mountain National Park's shorter winters are also having a devastating impact on the park's pine trees. The park's long, cold winters are necessary to kill bark beetles. These beetles spread a deadly fungus to pine trees. The beetles are thriving in the park's warmer climate, causing more pine trees to die.

While park rangers cannot stop climate change, they can reduce its effects. Park rangers in Rocky Mountain National Park apply insecticides to trees to keep the beetles away and prune any parts of trees that show signs of the fungus. Park workers also collect pine seeds and plant seedlings to help restore parts of the park devastated by pine beetles.

Another species affected by climate change is the pika. These small mammals live above the tree line in alpine regions where temperatures rarely rise above freezing. If the temperature reaches 78 degrees Fahrenheit (26°C), pikas can overheat and die. Unlike other mountain species that can move to higher areas to cool off, many pikas are already at the highest elevations in the park. There is often no place for them to go. Although pika populations are stable now, park rangers warn that the animals could

PERSPECTIVES

MAKING AN ENVIRONMENTALLY FRIENDLY PARK

Rocky Mountain National Park staff are working to make the park more environmentally friendly. Staff use electric vehicles and limit the amount of energy used to power buildings in the park. Paul McLaughlin is a scientist at the park. He says that he hopes these steps "encourage the larger community to reduce their impacts that are facilitating climate change."

THE ROCKY PLEDGE

I pledge to . . .

Build safe fires

Drive on designated areas

Dispose of waste properly

Watch wildlife from a distance

Take nothing from the park

Keep pets leashed and in designated areas

Respect and protect all public lands

The Rocky Pledge outlines ways visitors can protect Rocky Mountain National Park. How do these actions protect the park? Are there other ways visitors can protect the park?

die out over the next 50 years if the park's temperatures continue to rise. Scientists are monitoring the park's pikas to find ways to protect the animals.

THE ROCKY PLEDGE

Visitors play an important role in protecting Rocky Mountain National Park. One way tourists can help conserve the park is by taking the Rocky Pledge. Visitors who take this pledge promise to protect the park and other public lands during their visits.

Rocky Mountain National Park is one of the top tourist destinations in the United States. The park's rich history, stunning natural environments, diverse species, and range of recreational activities make it unique. Protecting this park and caring for the environment will help ensure future generations can enjoy this spectacular region.

EXPLORE ONLINE

Chapter Five talks about climate change. The article at the website below goes into more depth on this topic. Does the article answer any of the questions you had about climate change? What questions do you still have?

GUIDE TO CLIMATE CHANGE

abdocorelibrary.com/rocky-mountain-national-park

PARK LANDMARKS

Deer Mountain is one of the easiest mountains to climb in the park. It offers views of Moraine Park and Longs Peak.

Moraine Park is a wide-open plain. It is one of the best places in the park for wildlife viewing.

Holzwarth Historic Site is an old ranch in Kawuneeche Valley. Visitors can tour the ranch to see what life was like for early settlers.

Forest Canyon Overlook is a scenic spot on Trail Ridge Road. The overlook offers panoramic views of the park.

Sky Pond is considered one of the best hikes in the park. The hike offers stunning views of mountains, waterfalls, and lakes.

Alberta Falls is one of the most visited attractions in the park. The waterfall is 30 feet (9 m) tall.

STOP AND THINK

Surprise Me

Chapter Two explores the geologic and human history of Rocky Mountain National Park. After reading this book, what two or three facts about the park's early history did you find most surprising? Write a few sentences about each fact. Why did you find each fact surprising?

Dig Deeper

After reading this book, what questions do you still have about Rocky Mountain National Park? With an adult's help, find a few reliable sources that can help you answer your questions. Write a paragraph about what you learned.

Say What?

Studying national parks can mean learning a lot of new vocabulary. Find five words in this book you've never heard before. Use a dictionary to find out what they mean. Then write the meanings in your own words, and use each word in a sentence.

You Are There

This book talks about the conservation efforts at Rocky Mountain National Park. Imagine you are a volunteer at the park. Write a letter home telling your friends about some of the projects you are involved in. Be sure to add plenty of details to your letter.

GLOSSARY

archaeologist
a person who studies human history

conservationist
a person who supports conservation, the protection of animals, plants, and natural resources

ecosystem
a community of organisms living together and interacting

erosion
the gradual wearing away of land by external forces, such as wind or water

glacier
a large, slow-moving body of ice

habitat
the natural home of a plant or animal

insecticide
a poison that kills or repels insects

picturesque
beautiful, resembling a photo or a painted scene

primeval
ancient

tectonic plate
one of the huge slabs of rock that form the earth's crust, the outermost layer of the planet

ONLINE RESOURCES

To learn more about Rocky Mountain National Park, visit our free resource websites below.

Visit **abdocorelibrary.com** or scan this QR code for free Common Core resources for teachers and students, including vetted activities, multimedia, and booklinks, for deeper subject comprehension.

Visit **abdobooklinks.com** or scan this QR code for free additional online weblinks for further learning. These links are routinely monitored and updated to provide the most current information available.

LEARN MORE

Lassieur, Allison. *The National Parks Encyclopedia*. Abdo, 2023.

USA National Parks. DK, 2024.

INDEX

About the Author

Heather C. Hudak has written hundreds of books for children on all kinds of topics. When Heather is not writing, she enjoys traveling and has been to more than 60 countries. Heather lives in the foothills of the Rocky Mountains. She has spent countless hours camping, wildlife watching, and exploring the many features of the land.